Plastic

Dana Meachen Rau

mc **Marshall Cavendish**
Benchmark
New York

To the students of East Farms Elementary School, Farmington, Connecticut
—D.M.R.

With thanks to Professor Keith Sheppard, Department of Chemical Engineering & Materials Science, Stevens Institute of Technology, Hoboken, New Jersey, for the careful review of this manuscript

Other Marshall Cavendish Offices:
Marshall Cavendish International (Asia) Private Limited, 1 New Industrial Road, Singapore 536196 • Marshall Cavendish International (Thailand) Co Ltd. 253 Asoke, 12th Flr, Sukhumvit 21 Road, Klongtoey Nua, Wattana, Bangkok 10110, Thailand • Marshall Cavendish (Malaysia) Sdn Bhd, Times Subang, Lot 46, Subang Hi-Tech Industrial Park, Batu Tiga, 40000 Shah Alam, Selangor Darul Ehsan, Malaysia

Marshall Cavendish is a trademark of Times Publishing Limited.

All websites were available and accurate when this book was sent to press.

Editor: Christina Gardeski
Publisher: Michelle Bisson
Art Director: Anahid Hamparian
Series Designer: Virginia Pope

Printed in Malaysia
1 3 5 6 4 2

Library of Congress Cataloging-in-Publication Data
Rau, Dana Meachen, 1971—
Plastic / Dana Meachen Rau.
p. cm. — (Use it! reuse it!)
Includes bibliographical references and index.
Summary: "Examines how we use plastic in everyday objects, its unique traits and qualities, and how it is processed to be useful to us. Also discusses how plastic can be recycled to use again"— Provided by publisher.
ISBN 978-1-60870-518-4 (print)
ISBN 978-1-60870-774-4 (ebook)
1. Plastics—Juvenile literature.
2. Plastics—Recycling—Juvenile literature.
I. Title.
CURR TA455.P5R29 2012
620.1'923—dc22
2010050200

Photo research by Connie Gardner

Cover photo by Garry Gay/Alamy

The photographs in this book are used by permission and through the courtesy of: *Alamy*: p. 3 Garry Gay; p. 9(B) Nick Young; p. 12 Andrew Patterson; p. 20(B) Phil Degginger; p. 21(B) Tricia de Courey Ling. *The Image Works*: p. 5(T) Bob Daemmrich; p. 9(T) NMPFT/DHA/SSPL. *AP Photo*: p. 10(R), p. 13(T). *Corbis*: pp. 4, 7(B), 8, 17 Encyclopedia; p. 5(B) Richard Schultz; p. 10(L) Bettmann. *Superstock*: pp. 1, 6, 15, 20(L) age fotostock; p. 7(T) Index Stock; p. 14 Flirt; p. 19 Blend Images. *Getty Images*: p. 11 DK Stock/Guillermo Hung; pp. 13(B), 16 Bloomberg; p. 18 Albert Lieal; p. 20(TR) Jeffrey Coolidge; p. 21(T) Tom Vezo.

Plastic

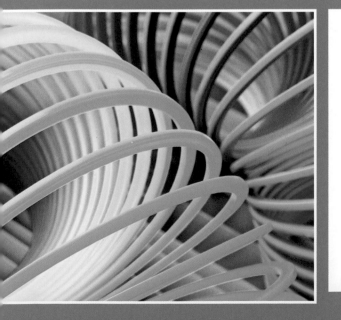

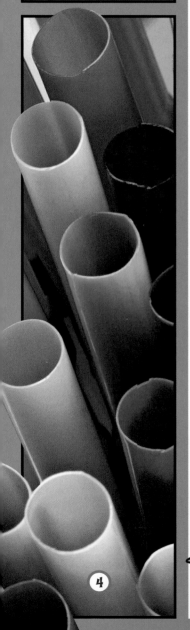

Chapter 1

The word plastic means "easily molded." Plastic can be formed into many shapes.

4

Everywhere You Look

What are you wearing today? You might be wearing plastic! Some jackets, socks, and backpacks are made from plastic. You may be wearing a hat or headband made from plastic. Your sneakers and bike helmet may have plastic parts, too.

Plastic can be clear or colorful. It can be stiff or bendy. Plastic doesn't weigh a lot, but it can be strong. It is easily formed into shapes. For all of these reasons, plastic is a good material to make many of the things we use every day.

Both your umbrella and your raincoat are made of plastic.

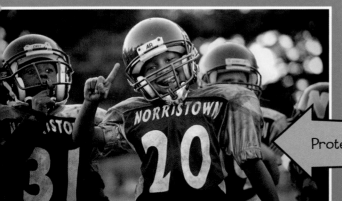

Protect your head with a plastic helmet.

The bristles of a hairbrush are made of plastic.

We use a lot of plastic. Plastic containers in the kitchen hold salsa, cookies, and nuts. Plastic bottles hold water, soda, and ketchup. In the bathroom, a plastic bottle holds shampoo. You brush your hair with a plastic brush and rinse your mouth with a plastic cup. You sit on a plastic toilet seat.

In school, you write with a plastic pen or markers. You toss your trash into a plastic trash bin. Maybe your lunch is wrapped in plastic wrap. Perhaps you play with a kickball or a board game with plastic pieces. Plastic is truly everywhere!

People who lived long ago did not use plastic. They used wood, stone, pottery, and metal to make everyday items they needed.

Many items in your classroom, including markers, have plastic parts.

Plastic containers can hold your lunch. You can clean them and reuse them every day.

Scientists discovered all of the natural things on Earth are made up of **chemicals**. People realized they could mix, change, and heat chemicals. The chemicals could be turned into new substances. That's how plastic was invented. Over time, people invented many types of plastics that could be used in different ways.

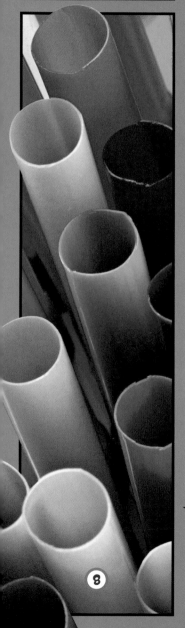

Bakelite was one of the first most widely used plastics because it could be molded into many shapes.

A New Material

This dough-like plastic was made into toothbrushes at this early plastic factory.

Plastic was invented in 1855 by Alexander Parkes. He called it Parkesine. That first plastic was later called **celluloid**. In the late 1800s, inventors tried mixing different chemicals to make something new. This is how John Wesley Hyatt improved celluloid. It could be heated, and then molded into shape. When it cooled, it became hard.

But the first plastic to have success across the world was Bakelite. Invented in 1907, Bakelite could be molded and hardened into any shape. It was light and strong. Bakelite was used to make furniture, telephones, radios, and jewelry.

Bakelite bangle bracelets

People found many uses for plastic, from airplane parts to children's records.

More people experimented with chemicals to make more types of plastic. In the 1940s during World War II plastic was used for airplane parts because it was light and easily formed into smooth shapes. **Vinyl** could be used to cover wires. **Nylon** was used for parachutes and ropes.

Soon, many household items that had been made from wood, metal, cotton, and glass could be made from plastic, too. People stored food in plastic containers and wrapped food in plastic wrap. They listened to music on plastic records. Women wore nylon stockings. Kids played with plastic toys and dolls. People brushed with plastic toothbrush bristles. Before, bristles had been made from animal hair.

In the 1960s, astronauts explored space for the first time. Plastic was used, and is still used, to make spacecraft parts because it is light and strong.

Plastic has uses in almost every **industry**. Computers, televisions, and many other machines have plastic parts. Plastic became an important building material, too. It is used to make siding, doors, countertops, floors, and water pipes.

Today, we use plastic when we communicate with each other with cell phones. We use plastic to get around in cars, bikes, and airplanes. We paint with plastic paint, dress with plastic buttons, and play with plastic hula hoops. Plastics play a part in many things we do.

Plastic siding covers the outside of a house. You can play with a plastic hula hoop on the sidewalk.

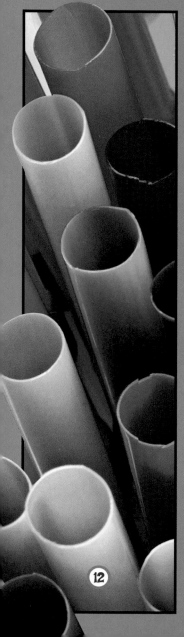

Chapter 3

12

Plastic can be made into all sorts of bright colors.

Made from Molds

The main ingredients in plastics come from oil and natural gas, found deep underground. Chemical companies heat this oil and gas to break apart the chemicals inside them. They link the chemicals together in new ways to form **resins**. These resins can be used to make plastic.

Workers drill deep into the ground for natural gas.

Plastic companies make resins in many forms. They can be tiny round pellets, grainy powders, or large sheets. They sell these resins to other companies that make them into the

Resins are sometimes made into small round shapes called pellets.

products we use. Chemicals, colors, and other ingredients may be added to the resins along the way, depending on what the factory needs to make.

Many plastic products are formed by heating resins until they melt. Then the melted plastic is put into a **mold**. As the plastic cools, it gets hard. It takes the shape of the mold.

This can happen many different ways. In blow molding, a machine pours resin into a mold. Then air blows in. The resin moves to

Plastic resins are heated until they melt.

Melted plastic is poured into molds. It cools into shapes, such as building blocks.

the sides of the mold so the inside is hollow. That's how plastic bottles are made. To make a playground ball, a round mold spins. The resin pushes to the sides of the mold. Sometimes resin is **injected** into a mold. That's how plastic building blocks are made.

Flat plastic for a tablecloth is made by squeezing hot plastic between two rollers. A tube of plastic is made by pushing resin through

Some plastic runs through rollers to make it flat.

a hole. Pressure and heat work together to mold other products. A plastic sheet can be pushed or sucked down into a mold. That's how a plastic bathtub is made.

Sometimes, workers at a factory add bubbles of air into the resin. The plastic gets foamy and hardens. It is used to make softer plastic products, like seat cushions.

Some types of plastics, such as **epoxy**, cannot be shaped by melting the way other plastics can. Instead, chemicals are combined right in a mold. The chemicals react to each other and form the hard epoxy. As the plastic forms, it takes the shape of the mold. Boats and tennis rackets are made this way. Thin fibers, or threads, of glass are sometimes added to the plastic to make a substance called fiberglass, which is much stronger than epoxy alone. So many products are made of plastic!

This fiberglass boat is made by mixing plastic with thin threads of glass.

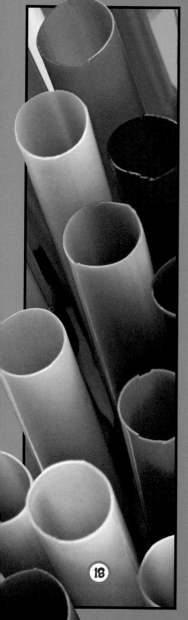

Chapter 4

Too much trash! Plastic piles up with garbage at a landfill.

18

The Plastic Problem

Plastic is an important part of our lives. But there is a problem with plastic.

Many of the things we throw away are brought to **landfills**. Over time, most of the trash in a landfill will turn to soil. But it can take some plastics hundreds or even thousands of years to **decompose**. Plastic litter on the ground won't decompose either. It can get washed into rivers and oceans. It floats around for a very long time. Animals can get tangled in it.

Instead of throwing plastic away, we can recycle it!

Throw your plastic into a recycling bin instead of a garbage can.

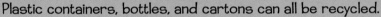
Plastic containers, bottles, and cartons can all be recycled.

You may have a recycling bin that you put outside for a truck to pick up. Or you can bring **recyclables** right to a local recycling center. In some states, you can bring plastic bottles back to grocery stores and trade them in for money.

At the recycling center, workers and machines sort the plastics. They

20 Recycled shredded plastic can be used to make new products.

send them to companies to reuse them. Some plastics can be melted again. They are made into new products, like water bottles, flower pots, traffic cones, or thread for socks. Some plastics can't be melted again. But they can be shredded and used for the filling for sleeping bags or **artificial** grass on sports fields.

Recycling centers may not be able to recycle every type of plastic. So you need to think of ways you can reuse plastic yourself. Use a plastic grocery bag again. Make juice or water bottle tops into an interesting craft. Turn a milk jug into a bird feeder!

People have found many uses for plastic. You can look for ways to reuse plastic, too!

Be creative with plastic! What can you make with some old plastic pots?

21

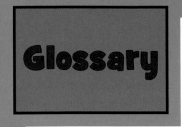
Glossary

artificial [ahr-tuh-FISH-uhl] made by people, not by nature

celluloid [SEL-yuh-loid] an early plastic-like substance made from cellulose, a material found in wood

chemicals [KEM-i-kuhls] substances found in the earth or created by mixing, heating, or changing them

decompose [dee-kuhm-POHZ] to break down into basic parts and turn into soil

epoxy [ih-POK-see] resin mixed with a hardener, used to make plastic products such as tennis rackets, or used to glue other materials together

industry [IN-duh-stree] a group of workers, factories, and businesses in a related field that makes a product or provides a service

injected [in-JEKT-ed] to push or force something into a hole or mold

landfills [LAND-fils] areas of land set aside for layers of trash and soil

mold [MOHLD] a hollow form used to make an object by filling it with a material that takes the shape of the form

nylon [NAHY-lon] a type of plastic that can be made into fabric and is used to make jackets, backpacks, stockings, carpets, ropes, and many other products

recyclables [ree-SAHY-kluh-buhls] items that can be made into products again

resins [REZ-ins] substances made by linking chemicals in a certain way

vinyl [VAHYN-I] a type of plastic, also known as PVC, that can be stiff or soft, and is used for pipes, raincoats, and many other products

Books to Discover

Barraclough, Sue. *A Plastic Toy*. Milwaukee, WI: Gareth Stevens Publishing, 2006.

Fix, Alexandra. *Reduce, Reuse, Recycle: Plastic*. Chicago, IL: Heinemann Educational, 2007.

Inches, Alison. *The Adventures of a Plastic Bottle: A Story about Recycling*. New York: Little Simon, 2009.

Langley, Andrew. *Everyday Materials: Plastic*. NY: Crabtree Publishing, 2008.

Ross, Kathy. *Look What You Can Make with Plastic Bottles and Tubs*. Honesdale, PA: Boyds Mills Press, 2002.

Websites to Explore

American Chemistry: Plastics
www.americanchemistry.com/s_plastics/index.asp

Earth 911: Plastic
http://earth911.com/recycling/plastic

4 2 Explore: Recycle-Reduce-Reuse
www.42explore.com/recycle.htm

35+ Uses for Plastic Milk Jugs
www.plantea.com/milk-jug.htm

Index

About the Author

Dana Meachen Rau is the author of more than 250 books for children. She has written about many nonfiction topics from her home office in Burlington, Connecticut. Dana is grateful for plastic, because without it, she couldn't snuggle in her favorite fleece blanket!

With thanks to the Reading Consultants:

Nanci R. Vargus, Ed.D., is an Assistant Professor of Elementary Education at the University of Indianapolis.

Beth Walker Gambro is an Adjunct Professor at the University of Saint Francis in Joliet, Illinois.

Franklin Pierce University

00194458

DATE DUE